The

Unbelievable

Ikigai Book

Happiness Express For Swift

Self-Improvement Secrets

Hiroto Niura

Imprint

© Copyright 2024: Copyright notice

Self-publisher: Hiroto Niura

Cover design: Patrick Hohensee

Represented by: PH Digital Publishing

Contact: Patrick Hohensee

Contact: Patrick Hohensee Wiesbadener Str. 59B, 14197 Berlin

Website: https://www.patrick-hohensee.de/en

For questions and comments

E-Mail: contact@patrick-hohensee.de

Blog for further education on Self Improvement:

https://www.patrick-hohensee.de/en/blog

Thank You

We are delighted that you have chosen this book to begin your journey of self-improvement. We truly appreciate the trust you've placed in us. In this guide, we will help you find your path to happiness and self-improvement. As lifelong learners ourselves, we believe that books are powerful tools for growth.

Your honest feedback is invaluable. It helps us improve this book and create even better resources for future readers. We would be truly grateful if you could give us an honest and objective review after completing your Ikigai journey.

We hope you enjoy reading and gain valuable insights from this guide. Happy reading

Warm regards,
Hiroto Niura & Patrick Hohensee

This Book belongs to:

_____

_____

Your Name

"Don't dwell on the past,

don't dream of the future.

Concentrate on the present moment."

- Buddha -

Preface

We rush from one appointment to the next; our calendars are jam-packed with personal and professional appointments, and we barely have time for what really matters to us. We live a life that doesn't fulfill us.

This is how my life was a few years ago. I dragged myself to the office in the morning and sat tired in front of the TV late at night — exhausted from the daily grind. It seemed as if the weeks were repeating themselves, and I was excited about the weekend every week. I felt increasingly burned out and distanced from myself, as if I were idling. After several years on the hamster wheel, a spontaneous short vacation opened my eyes, and I knew that things couldn't go on like this. I asked myself a question that changed my life: What am I living for?

Perhaps you, too, are searching for your true purpose. Questions such as "What is life" or "What is my calling" do not let you rest, and you sense that something is not right in your life. The daily autopilot makes you tired, and you wish you had time again for the things you truly enjoy.

Only a few people do what they like. We might think that they are an exception. But hand in hand, aren't we all born to make the most of this life? Wouldn't it be a shame to waste this precious time on something that neither fulfills us nor brings us joy?

The Japanese philosophy of life, "Ikigai," is dedicated to questions like these. It can be translated as "what is worth living for" The Asian way of life is an intelligent concept with which we can learn how to find new inspiration for our lives. Which activities suit me, and what are my strengths and weaknesses?

Japanese companies, personalities, and artists have been drawing on this concept for many years and using the philosophy of life to find the inner motivation for their work and lives. According to Japanese tradition, everyone carries an ikigai within them and can find it by searching for themselves. In the western world, this concept is challenging to find. I would therefore like to introduce you to the concept of ikigai.

With this book, you have already taken the first step towards a new life. You know that things can't go on like this. I felt the same way many years ago and started with my new perspective. As a result, I was given more time for the things I really wanted to do!

If these words resonate with you, read on and find out how you too can find your Ikigai. Find the true calling for your life and live in fulfillment. Day by day.

1. How it all began

"There is no path to happiness.
Happiness is the way."
(Buddha)

The Japanese island of Okinawa is widely regarded as the island of longevity, as its inhabitants possess the highest life expectancy in the world. They live for around a hundred years, and some even longer. The Ikigai way of life is widespread among the inhabitants.

They take this concept to heart and act for their ikigai in their everyday lives. The small village of Ogimi in northern Okinawa, with around 3,000 inhabitants, is particularly well-known for its beautiful sea views, slow-paced everyday life, its many vegetable gardens, and the numerous gatherings of its inhabitants.

But above all, it is the inhabitants themselves who make the village seem almost like something from another world. People are happy with what they do and always wear a smile on their faces. There are also fewer chronic diseases, and the dementia rate is lower than the global average. The inhabitants of Ogimi live by the way of life:

"You are young at 80. If your ancestors invite you to heaven when you're 90, ask them to wait until you're 100.
When you are 100 years old, you may change your mind".

Okinawa is not the only place where people are happy with their lives and see things from a different perspective. Sardinia (Italy), Nicoya (Costa Rica), Ikaria (Greece) and Loma Linda (California, USA) are also special places. Life is lived there differently. They are also known as the "Blue Zones". What makes these places so special, and what do they have in common?

1.1 HARA HACHI BU — EAT WISELY

Let's take a closer look at Okinawa and the lives of its inhabitants. The diet of the inhabitants of Okinawa consists primarily of fruit and vegetables. They also eat more fish than meat. True to the motto "Let your food be your medicine" (Nuchi gusui), the inhabitants eat sweet potatoes, bitter melons, seaweed, green leafy vegetables and fresh fruit. Many of these foods contain important nutrients that are considered anti-inflammatory and prevent oxidative stress. As a result, they consume fewer calories than people in the western regions of the world.

The words "Hara Bachi Bu" can be translated as "Eat wisely". It is a typical phrase in Okinawa, according to which people eat every day. Instead of eating as much as possible at every meal, they leave room in their stomachs.

They fill their stomachs to around 80 percent and still have some space. The inhabitants have found tricks with which they can maintain this eating habit, such as eating from a smaller plate.

1.2 IKIGAI — A REASON TO GET UP IN THE MORNING

Far removed from Western society, the people of Okinawa lead a way of life that we can learn from here. In addition to a healthy diet for more vitality, the focus is primarily on the meaning of life. The inhabitants have a reason for which they live and perform their daily work. All actions therefore have a purpose, and people wake up in the morning with a meaning for their lives. They carry out their responsibilities with this in mind, such as working in the fields, looking after the children, or cooking for the family.

Family and community are also vital in Okinawa. Social life is well-structured. They allow themselves to flow with life and do not pay much attention to time. Instead, they trust that time is on their side.

In this way, you too can give your life meaning. And prolong it at the same time! The healthy lifestyle of the inhabitants of Okinawa and the other Blue Zones, where a similar lifestyle is practiced, shows a higher life expectancy among the inhabitants.

Enhance your life through little mindful actions. In this way, you can give meaning to each day and create the Blue Zone within yourself. Here are a few suggestions on how to find your Ikigai:

- Go out into nature every day.
- Spend time in silence.
- Offer to help your neighbors (e.g., with grocery shopping or yard repairs).
- Make healthy choices in your diet (e.g., an apple instead of a piece of cake).
- Eat less rather than too much, and leave room in your stomach.
- Show gratitude and say "thank you" (e.g., when someone holds the door open for you).

By bringing more balance into your life, you will also feel more harmonious with yourself and your environment. In this way, you will go through life more easily and learn to flow with it. Like the inhabitants of the Blue Zones, you too will feel better all around.

Part 1: Self-reflection—do a self-check!

— What activities and events cause me stress?

— Am I often aggressive and annoyed? Which activities and events trigger these emotions?

For the next 5 days: Observe your emotions. When do you react angrily or emotionally? Instead of reacting as usual, pause and observe the emotion and thoughts. Then ask yourself, What has changed?

Practice Mindfulness: Do you act consciously in everyday life, or do you work as if programmed? Consciously carry out three actions from everyday life. Give them your full attention without allowing yourself to be distracted (e.g., by a phone call or a glance at your cell phone). Examples: Brushing your teeth in the morning, drinking your coffee or cooking dinner.

2. The Supporting Pillars of Ikigai

The word ikigai comes from Japanese and describes a Japanese philosophy of life. There is no direct word that can be used to translate ikigai. Instead, we can only guess what it means.

The word part "iki" means "life," and "gai" can be translated as "value". It therefore means something like "life value".

Or in a nutshell:

That which is worth living for
or what is worth getting up for in the morning.

With our ikigai, we give life an interpretation and a more in-depth meaning. You learn to live in the moment and make fewer plans for the future. This is what the principle of Ikigai teaches you every day: always live in the moment and less in the future or past. This puts less strain on the brain and leads to the regeneration of brain and skin cells. Various studies have shown that stress can have various health consequences, such as digestive and cardiovascular problems. Our skin cells are also affected by high-stress levels in everyday life and age more quickly. In addition, higher stress levels in the modern age lead to an increase in psychological difficulties such as burnout and depression.

Ikigai shows you how to escape the stress trap and achieve greater longevity. Let's focus on the details of Ikigai:

1) Start small. Focus on the details.

2) Surrender to life: Accept who you are.

3) Balance and sustainability: Trust others.

4) The joy of small things: Enjoy your five senses.

5) Live in the moment: Find your flow.

Start your new life today and change small details in your everyday life. It could be consciously brushing your teeth or going for a walk in the morning instead of ignoring the alarm clock several times as usual. Start your day right, and you will learn to live your life again.

1. Start small. Focus on the details.

The first pillar of Ikigai shows that it is the little things in life that count. Okinawans know this too. They worry about the small needs in life. Instead of having a big goal in mind, they focus on the things they do. Artists have made this their philosophy of life. Their works of art are created by indulging currently and not having the result in mind.

- ☐ Do one thing and put aside your tendency to multitask.
- ☐ When you write an E-Mail, focus only on the E-Mail.
- ☐ Pay attention to how you live your day and turn down the autopilot.

2. **Accept who you are.**

Are you living your life in fear and anxiety? Then it's time you looked at it from a different perspective. Use this life and your talents. Instead of comparing yourself to others as usual, accept yourself. In this way, you will find your Ikigai more easily and create what you are made for.

- ☐ Write a list of your talents.
- ☐ Take up a new hobby that you have always wanted to do.
- ☐ Do something you are usually afraid of (e.g., traveling alone).

3. Balance and sustainability: Trust nature.

Nature has set everything in motion, and we can trust it. Today's modern man has largely forgotten how to live with nature. Spend time in nature every day, like in your garden or in the forest. Get to know the environment and start with a vegetable garden or growing herbs on your balcony. You will see that working in nature grounds and calms us humans.

- ☐ Spend some time in nature every day.
- ☐ Grow vegetables, fruit, or herbs.
- ☐ Recycle your waste and watch what you use.

4. The joy of small things: Enjoy your five senses.

Taste, touch, hearing, sight and smell. The five senses are innate to us by nature. However, we often misuse them. Too loud music, too much food or too many words are all part of modern people's lives. We lose our balance and allow ourselves to drift away from our senses instead of consciously perceiving them. Try an experiment and consciously use your sensory organs:

- ☐ Taste the different spices in your food.
- ☐ Listen carefully to your friends and colleagues.
- ☐ Smell your food before you devour it.
- ☐ Feel textiles and surfaces, like the warm fur of a cat or the soft texture of your comforter.
- ☐ Look at nature, like a butterfly in the garden or a buzzing bee on a plant.

5. Find your flow.

We humans tend to wallow in the future or the past. We miss what's happening right now. Likewise, we ignore the birds singing in the garden, the rippling of the water as we wash the dishes, or the engine of the car. Instead, we listen to our thoughts. Surrender to this moment, and don't think about the past or future as usual.

- ☐ What do you notice at this moment?
- ☐ Stop for 1-2 minutes and pause if you have too much stress or feel overwhelmed by your work.
- ☐ What do you hear when you let your thoughts go?

An important factor in Ikigai is work.

People in Okinawa work every day and it is part of their everyday life. They keep themselves busy and can also keep their bodies moving. At the same time, various happiness hormones are activated and work becomes a joy. Instead of separating work from the fun in life, the boundaries of fun and work merge into one another. In other words: work and passion meet and become one.

If you integrate these five pillars into your life, you will bring your life into balance. Do you work too much? You can learn to work less and gain more time for what you really want to do. If you don't enjoy your job, you can find your vocation and earn money doing what you enjoy. Ikigai guides us to rediscover our essence and align our passions with the world's needs.

If you don't enjoy your work and do your job according to routine or your boss's instructions, then you can make a change. Here and now! Because you are the master or mistress of your life. Make it your resolution to find your Ikigai and live out of it. Not only will you feel freer, but you will also enjoy your work more and enjoy the little things in life again.

Let's take an example at this point to illustrate Ikigai in everyday Western life:

Shortly before I resigned from my job, I was up to my neck in work. I was overwhelmed, both professionally and privately. Neither my job as a permanent employee nor my private life were going as I wanted. My relationship was a disaster, and I was hiding at work. My health was on the edge, and I was on the verge of burnout. My job didn't allow me to take a vacation, which I took anyway. The short vacation came at just the right time, and I am grateful that I answered the call. Because this vacation was going to change my life completely.

When I decided to quit my job, an inner knot loosened. It was as if I could breathe again and meet life with open arms. The last few months at work were relaxed, and I was excited about my new freedom. I was sure that I would now be doing something that I was passionate about and that I loved doing from the bottom of my heart. So I set off on a long journey into the wide world.

Are you interested in pursuing your authentic purpose? Then listen to your Ikigai and untie the inner knot. Do what you were born to do and stop hiding!

Part 2: Self-reflection—do the self-check!
- What do you enjoy doing?
- What could the world need from you?
- How could you earn money with it?
- What are your strengths and talents?

3. Dealing with Problems

"Sit still — do nothing.
Spring is coming,
the grass grows by itself."
(Zen Mantra)

Illustrate the following situation: A surfer is standing on his surfboard and surfing the high, turbulent waves of an ocean. He requires intense concentration to stay on his surfboard and avoid vanishing into the ocean depths. When observing a surfer, we notice their unwavering focus on the present. He cannot allow himself to be distracted for a single moment.

19

If the surfer is swept along by a wave, he falls into the water and has to get up again. He cannot remain lying down. Otherwise, he would be carried away by the flowing water. The surfer will therefore get back on his surfboard as quickly as possible and ride the waves. We see a similar process, particularly often with children, when they are learning to walk or ride a bike. They fall down and get up again. This can happen up to a hundred times. But the child gets up again.

What do you do in a problem situation? Do you stay down, or do you get up again? Just like the surfer in the wild ocean or the child taking their first steps, you too must learn to get up again. This is especially true when you are faced with a difficulty and have to overcome it. But how can you always stay currently and focus all your attention on it? Hide from a difficulty; just put it off. Instead of starting your job search right away, postpone it from day to day. This way, you stay with the current job that you don't like.

We also skillfully put off small everyday concerns. At this point, take a moment to reflect and ask yourself:

What issue do I need to solve, and what am I putting off?

You are sure to find one or more concerns that you are putting off. We humans are used to putting off difficulties instead of tackling them. If we now look at the Japanese way of life, we learn to tackle difficulties— here and now! Because in Ikigai there is no future. The Japanese always live at the moment. At the same time, they know that difficulties arise in helping them. We can grow from issues and learn from them. However, we can only do this if we face them. A child who loses courage during his first attempts on a bicycle and remains lying on the ground will never learn to ride a bicycle. Concerns, therefore, help our development. Instead of being intimidated by the issue, we face it and can feel bigger as a result.

Ikigai teaches us to accept this moment with everything that is. This includes issues, crises, and challenges. The people of Okinawa dedicate themselves to their work and the issues that arise every day. They do not complain and accept challenges with a smile. They do not wallow in the past or the future. Instead of reacting to the difficulty, let it sink in. This helps you find a solution easier.

Let's take a step-by-step approach to overcoming the problem:

1. Focus on a single task.
2. Give yourself completely to your work / activity.
3. Do not allow yourself to be distracted when an issue arises.

Approach the problem in this way:

- How much is it bothering you now?
- How much will it still bother you in a week's time?
- How much will it bother you in a month's time?
- How much will it bother you in a year's time?

Look at the difficulty from a distance, and you will realize that the concern no longer seems as big as it initially appeared.

We can illustrate the Japanese way of thinking with a practical example: Mr. Bauer is a master baker in Berlin and has to produce 1,500 baked goods in three days for a large event. He is a modest baker and normally only fulfills smaller orders. His time for baking the baked goods is limited, and he is under pressure. How can the Ikigai concept help Mr. Bauer?

Before Mr. Bauer starts baking, he asks himself the following questions:

1) How big is the difficulty **now?**
2) How much will the big project still be on my mind in **a week's time?**
3) How busy will I be in **a month's time?**
4) How busy will I be in **a year's time?**

Now, Mr. Bauer can distance himself from his issue and realize that it will be solved in a week's time.

If Mr. Bauer thinks about the issue in a month or even a year, he will probably laugh about it. Mr. Bauer can breathe a sigh of relief and find his way back to this moment.

In this way, he can devote his full attention to the baking project and finish it with a smile on his face.

Part 3: Self-reflection—Do the self-check!

Write down three major issues that you have been confronted with in the last few days. Then write down these four questions for each problem and answer them:

• Watch your feelings when dealing with the issue?

• How did you solve it?

• What did you learn from the difficulty and how you overcame it?

• Plan how to handle problems in the future based on what you learned in this chapter.

4. How Crises Can Help Us

"Learn to let go.
That is the key to happiness."
(Buddha)

We are all familiar with them—crises. Crises come out of nowhere and then disappear again. The inhabitants of the island state of Okinawa are particularly aware of this. They gratefully accept crises and see them as challenges through which they can learn and grow.

Crises are simply part of our lives. A death in the family, a conflict at work, an argument in a relationship, or a serious illness. We can look at them like a thunderstorm that comes and storms through the land. Once the storm has passed, everything becomes calm and quiet. A crisis usually has the same effect: before the crisis, everything was normal. During the crisis, however, everything is dark. After the crisis, everything is quiet again. But how can we keep a cool head during a crisis and perceive the silence?

The longer the crisis lasts, the more stress hormones are released. This causes the body to age more quickly. In addition, the immune system is more vulnerable than in a calm state. Finding your Ikigai will help you stay mentally strong and calm.

4.1 AN OPPORTUNITY

Many people have used a crisis as an opportunity to grow. Because crises come to you like cleansing thunderstorms that correct your mistakes. If you can look at it from this perspective, you will soon find more balance and harmony in your life.

After I resigned from my job and spent the first few months in South America, the money in my account dwindled. It came to a point where I had to start working. Days and weeks went by, and I didn't know which job would suit me. The money dwindled, and I knew that I would soon be destitute. One evening — at a campfire with friends, I decided: I wanted to draw portraits from now on. But how can you earn money from it?

Ikigai showed me that it's what we do in life that counts. After I turned my hobby into a profession, more and more people approached me and commissioned portraits. This allowed me to keep traveling and doing what I really loved. Instead of burying your head in the sand during a crisis, it's important to take an in-depth look inside yourself. Ask yourself the following questions, which have an important value in Ikigai:

What do I love, or what do I like to do?

Take a moment and look at what you like to do. Where do you find your passion, and what does your heart burn for? You must be honest with yourself. Because this is where your life begins anew. The Japanese value this question particularly highly and base their entire lives on it. This allows you to live and work in your Ikigai every day. This includes both professional and private life (such as family life, professional life, or family and community life). Doing what you love will influence everything else in your life.

What am I good at?

Use the crisis to find yourself again. Write down your strengths, such as openness or a willingness to learn. Do you love children and can't imagine life without them? Or are you good with technology? There is a saying in Japanese: "10 people, 10 colors." Every person is different and has different abilities. It's your job to find them within yourself!

What does the world need from me?

Or, to put it another way, what are you here for? What can you give back to the world? Once you have answered the first two questions for yourself, the answer to this question will also emerge from your heart. In this way, you will find your true calling, such as working with wood as a carpenter or working with shapes and colors as a graphic designer.

What can I be paid for?

In the last step, take a look at whether you can get paid for your chosen profession. As in my vocation as a portrait artist, you also have the chance to find something that you are paid for and that you love. In this way, you will naturally find your Ikigai, which will accompany you through life. There are things you love but can't get paid for, such as playing chess or doing somersaults. However, you can use the hobby as a basis for your career by developing your strategic and logical thinking or by staying active and sporty.

We recognize that a crisis offers you the opportunity to go deeper into yourself and find what you really want. This applies to both your professional and private lives. You can imagine your life as a flower that is held together by the core (Ikigai). The petals represent work, family, friends, sports, and hobbies. Each area influences the other and finds a more in-depth meaning in life through the Ikigai.

Japanese culture shows us by example that it is worth seeing every crisis as an opportunity. The ability to innovate and creativity find new value, and the Japanese allow themselves to flow with life and its ups and downs. Can you live this way too?

Part 4: Self-Reflection. Do the self-check!

Where do you find your motivation for your life? Instead of looking at a crisis from a negative perspective, use the crisis to your advantage. Every crisis comes for a reason! Ask yourself these questions to help you deal with difficulties:

1. What is the point of your life?
2. What do you live for?
3. Do you do what you love in your everyday life?
4. What positive impact would you like to make on the world?
5. What do you do in a crisis?

For the next 3 days:

☐ **Write an Ikigai diary.**

Sit down every evening for 5–10 minutes and write down what you have done that day. Read the entries after three days and analyze what you would like to change in your everyday life.

☐ **Analyze your day:**

Do you act out of habit or compulsion? When do you do the things in your everyday life with passion?

Where is there resistance within you?

How do you act in a crisis?

☐ **Changes to your everyday life:**

This could be certain actions (e.g., smoking) or relationships (e.g., with negative friends).

5. Kaizen (改善) — Change for the Better

"He who knows contentment is truly rich,

even without material possessions."

(Nagarjuna)

Kaizen is a Japanese method used to structure companies and organizations. It was first adopted by the Toyota Motor Corporation, which wanted to promise punctual production and delivery of its products.

However, companies such as Ford and Nestlé also adopted the Japanese principle to work in a more structured and innovative way. Kaizen is used particularly frequently in the production sector. Kaizen is also used by companies in other organizational areas such as software, education, healthcare, software development, and the media industry.

The meaning of the word Kaizen can be translated as "continuous improvement.". "Kai" means "change," and "Zen" means "good.". It is about successfully converting processes and resources in companies over the long term. The principle first emerged after the Second World War, when companies were recovering from the consequences of the war and had to restructure themselves. The successful conversion of companies such as Toyota made the principle of Kaizen known around the world.

But it is not only companies that have adopted Kaizen. Japanese people have also learned to get a better grip on their lives through Kaizen. Kaizen gives them a certain structure and security. Through the five pillars on which Kaizen is based, people can find a way to make their living environment safer and more harmonious. How can you integrate Kaizen into your life?

5.1 KAIZEN IN FOCUS

Kaizen consists of five parts that build on and merge into one another. We can also see them as the supporting pillars that keep Kaizen alive. These pillars are:

1) Seiri — Sorting

2) Seiton — Creating a visible structure

3) Seiso — Keep clean

4) Seiketsu — Standardize

5) Shitsuk — Securing and improving

You can implement these five steps (or: 5S movements) in your everyday life. By slowly making the change, you will work in a more structured way and improve your private environment. The Japanese are considered structured, orderly, and clean. They carry a certain image with them that you can also learn and adopt. With the 5S movements, you can take the first step towards a more productive life.

We can see this particularly well in the following examples:

1. Where can you find a better overview?
   An organized office or chaos on your desk and in your documents?
2. Where do you find more structure?
   In a tidy home or in unsorted shelves and cupboards?
3. Where do you find more harmony?
   In a clean room that is cleaned daily, or in an unclean home?
4. Where do you find more security?
   In the chaos of your calendar, or in a structured calendar that promises you breaks between appointments?
5. Where do you find satisfaction?
   In a daily routine filled with negative habits, or in a well-organized life?

Take a moment to look inside yourself. It is important to find your Ikigai.

So don't rush, and take your time. Remember life in the small village of Ogimi, where people live happily together and take time for the little things.

Sit down with a cup of tea and take as much time as you need.

5.2 THE 5S MODEL

Kaizen teaches you to harmonize your professional and private lives. Processes run harmoniously, and you can define clear goals. By constantly stopping and looking at your life, you will find a harmonious rhythm to your life and be able to set new goals.

1. Seiri (整理) — Sorting

A tidy home and a well-organized workplace are essential for keeping a clear head. By tidying up the places in our lives, we also cleanse ourselves from the inside. Our thoughts become clearer, and we can better define the goals of our lives. Take time to sort and tidy up! This process can also take an internal form, such as letting go of negative relationships or bad habits.

- ☐ Tidy up your house, apartment, and office and find the things you are looking for more easily.
- ☐ Reduce the risk of distraction from unnecessary things within your four walls.
- ☐ Make searching easier by tidying up regularly.
- ☐ Increase the security of your home by getting rid of unnecessary items.

2. Seiton (整頓) — Structure

The Seiton principle focuses on the places where you live and work. By keeping these places clean, you can work and live more productively. You also improve the flow of your work and living together with others, such as in a shared apartment or with family.

The more structured your life is, the more others will adapt too.

Ensure efficient organization of your living and work areas for easy access to all your essentials.

What do you use all the time, and what only sporadically? Sort things according to how often you use them.

Return items to their original position for easy retrieval.

Mark items so that you can recognize them at a glance (e.g., flour and sugar in the kitchen cupboard).

3. Seiso (清掃) — Keep clean

Keep your living environment clean. Put the dishes in the dishwasher, and put the laundry in the washing machine when it's time. Clean your house regularly, and do the same at your workplace. Prioritize this to prevent accidents and errors.

☐ Make your work and living areas safe by keeping them clean.

☐ Make sure that you can reach the areas easily.

☐ Do everything possible to ensure that you feel comfortable in your living areas.

☐ Clean regularly, and you will also find more space inside.

☐ Choose a day of the week to clean your rooms.

4. Seiketsu (清潔) — Standardize

Many people love individuality and want to make it as personal as possible. In the Japanese tradition, it is important to set a standard. Seiketsu ensures orderly work and living spaces.

- ☐ Clear slots in your calendar for practicing the 5S movements.
- ☐ Find a life and work structure that allows you to learn new practices (e.g., getting up earlier or doing yoga in the evening).
- ☐ Make new things a habit (like sweeping your kitchen daily or jogging through the park).
- ☐ Create a 5S to-do list that you can use to practice your new healthy habits (e.g., going for a walk every day).

5. Shitsuke (しつけ) – Self-Discipline

Only with self-discipline can we learn certain things. An artist can only become successful through discipline. Instead of allowing yourself to be distracted, you should therefore concentrate on the essentials. Well-known artists such as Leonardo Da Vinci and the Japanese writer Haruki Murakami also knew this.

- ☐ Organize your work steps when you start a new project.
- ☐ Set small goals that you can accomplish (e.g., work your side hustle before resigning from your day job).
- ☐ Look at the improvements in your process (e.g., jogging 5 km within 30 minutes).
- ☐ Identify the roots of problems instead of working around them and look for improvements.

Part 5: Self-reflection—do a self-check

Tidy up regularly and make life easier for yourself and those around you! Only take as much as you need, and let go of what you no longer need. This could be an old desk in the cellar or your grandfather's old vase that you neither use nor like.

What can't you let go of?
Write down five things that you can't let go of.

What offers you security?
Name the things that give you security (such as your family, the money in your bank account, etc.).

How structured is your life?
Be honest: do you live in inner and outer chaos, or do you live in a tidy and organized way? Which areas of your life can you tidy up?

Do you have self-discipline?
Do you allow yourself to be distracted by bad habits, or do you go through life with discipline? Name one bad habit that you want to stop today (e.g., smoking or surfing social

46

networks).

How do you work?

Do you work in chaos, or do you find the things you're looking for quickly? Take a few hours this week to structure your work environment (e.g., creating folders or deleting documents on your computer).

One brief reminder:

Have you ever wished to share the life-changing power of Ikigai with others?

Imagine someone who longs to feel energized and fulfilled but isn't sure where to start. Your review can be the spark they need! We believe everyone deserves access to self-improvement, and no one should miss out on the transformative power of Ikigai.

By sharing your thoughts on this book, you'll be extending a helping hand to fellow travelers on their path to personal growth. Your review could:

1. Inspire someone to embark on their own Ikigai journey.
2. Encourage a friend to make their well-being a priority.
3. Guide others towards a more vibrant and fulfilling life.
4. Ignite a passion for self-improvement and the wisdom of the East.

It takes just a moment to leave a review, but it could have a lasting impact on someone's life. So, why not share your experience and help others discover the life-changing power of Ikigai?

Ready to share your thoughts and join our supportive community?

How you submit a review:
1. Visit the Amazon product page.
2. Scroll down to the 'Customer Reviews' section.
3. Click on 'Write a customer review.'
4. Rate the book and write your review.
5. Click 'Submit.'

By sharing your experience, you're not just helping others; you're becoming part of something bigger. Welcome aboard!

We sincerely thank you for your support. Together, let's continue our journey to discover Ikigai and build vibrant, fulfilling lives!

6. Role Models

"Those who know the goal can decide.
Those who decide find peace.
Those who find peace are safe.
Those who are safe can reflect.
He who thinks can improve."
(Confucius)

In Japanese culture, the role of role models and mentors is vital. You can see this not only in the Japanese music scene, which thrives on pop stars and brings many fans with it. In the professional world, too, the connection to a mentor or role model is paramount.

Especially recently, mentor training has come to the fore in Japan. It allows protégé and mentor to work together, and the protégé can learn from the mentor.

However, such training could already be observed in Japan many centuries ago (especially in martial arts).

In this chapter, we would like to look at the role a mentor plays in the context of learning. Moreover, how can we learn from the Japanese and their contact with mentors? You may feel that you are not getting anywhere on your own and that you need the support of a mentor. You can get this support by connecting with a role model. Role models, even if not physically present, can serve as effective mentors—famous role models can also help.

6.1 MENTORSHIP

In Japan, the concept of Senpai-Kohai is considered in professional life. The word senpai means "superior" or "superordinate," and the part of the word "kohai" can be translated as "junior" or "subordinate". This already shows us what this concept is about: the connection between two people in which one person is subordinate to the other. Such a constellation can be found in many Japanese companies, organizations, businesses, and schools. For the sake of simplicity, we will use the terms "mentor" and "protégé".

What characterizes this concept above all is the impersonal touch in the connection between mentor and protégé. This may be due to the teachings' roots, which can be traced back to the Chinese philosopher Confucius. The teachings have been adopted from Japanese culture and have thus taken on a Japanese flavor. We can trace the Senpai-Kohai system back many centuries in Japanese history and see that the Civil Laws of 1898 also play an important role.

The specific role of a mentor has changed significantly lately. What originally developed naturally has now become a fixed training program in many companies. However, the mentor's tasks remain the same:

1. The mentor guides and protects his protégé.
2. The mentor helps in development.
3. He/She gives everything for the success of the protégé.

In this way, the protégé gets to know his strengths and weaknesses and is encouraged by his mentor. They feel empowered in their tasks and actions and can consult their mentor at any time. This gives them the security they need to achieve more success in their professional and private lives and to do what they really love.

How can this concept work and look in modern Western working life? A mentor is available to you around the clock and will ask you questions that make you think. You will learn to go deeper into yourself and find what really defines you.

Use the following mentoring questions to answer

them for yourself:

1. Do you have interests that you keep hidden (e.g., playing the piano, painting, dancing, or photography)?
2. What adventures are on your bucket list (e.g., go bungee jumping or go on a trip around the world)?
3. What have you always wanted to be but didn't do (e.g., wanting to be a dancer, mountain guide, or ski instructor)?

We can learn from another person in different ways. This can work in different ways, such as the mentor of a manager in the vegetable section of the supermarket or the mentor of a boxer. Trust, loyalty and empathy is crucial to find the right mentor.

As a mentor cannot always be physically present, you can also use the function of a role model for your success. Perhaps you know a person you admire and aspire to be like. Ask yourself:

1. What qualities do you admire in this individual?
2. How can you integrate the trait into your everyday life?
3. What is required for you to meet your goal?
4. How can your role model help you?

A mentor can be helpful at any age. What originated naturally in Japanese culture is now taking place in many Western companies. More and more employees, self-employed people and managers are finding a mentor at their side to help them define goals and achieve them. A mentor can help you identify your strengths and weaknesses. When we humans have a benchmark, we can manage our lives better and work more effectively.

6.2 LEADERSHIP

The Japanese concept of Senpai-Konhai is mainly found in Japanese schools. But you can also find mentoring programs in schools in this country, where the older students take care of the younger ones. Younger students learn from older peers and strive toward goals like joining sports teams or graduating. In Japanese schools, it is traditional for the younger students to take on everyday tasks, such as being the ball boy or washing the older students' school clothes. Attention is paid to respectful, polite and modest communication.

How can you use the senpai-kohai relationship for yourself if you have a role model to follow? By studying your role model closely, you can imitate their goals. Through their way of working and living, the role model shows you how you too can do what you love. Many well-known artists such as pop star Madonna, soccer star Cristiano Ronaldo or Facebook founder Mark Zuckerberg do exactly this. They have a certain amount of charisma and know what their strengths and weaknesses are. Analyze your role model:

Read the speeches of your role model:

- Read articles and speeches by and about your role model.
- Listen to podcasts and watch videos.

Analyze his or her appearance in public:

- What makes the role model special?
- What words does he or she use?
- What is his or her body language like?

Define the motivation of your role model:

- What motivates your role model?
- What does he/she do regularly (e.g., jog every morning)?
- What does he do without (e.g., eating meat)?

The better you understand your role model, the better you can understand him/her. You can adopt the goals of your role model and learn what you have to do. Therefore, make it your business to study the behavior of your role model and learn from him/her. A role model does not always have to be famous. Your supervisor, dad, or a close friend can also be helpful.

Part 6: Self-reflection. Do the self-check.

How can you learn from your role model? Use the following questions as a starting point:

Learning objective.

Begin by jotting down your desired areas of learning. Then write down what you can learn from your role model. This way, you can see how the role model can help you!

How can you integrate what you have learned into your everyday life?

☐ Do something every day for a week that your role model does. This way, you can also learn from him in practice and put what you have learned directly into practice. Here are some examples based on Steve Jobs:

☐ Get up thirty minutes earlier and meditate.

☐ Save yourself time in the morning and simplify your wardrobe.

☐ Shape your purpose in life through the things you love.

☐ Don't overeat and leave room in your stomach— remember the Japanese principle!

☐ Take a walk every day.

☐   Structure your everyday life.

What can you adopt in the long term?

New habits are easy to learn, but difficult to maintain. Therefore, start with two habits from your role model that you can adopt in your everyday life in the long term (more on this in chapter 8).

7. A Virtuous Life

"Tolerant means having strength,
to react to hatred and anger with understanding
and patience."
(Buddhist wisdom)

According to Japanese tradition, certain virtues are cultivated. From an early age, the Japanese are taught the importance of gratitude, diligence, and thrift. In this way, they learn not to complain and to be grateful for what they have. Take a look at the life of a Japanese person and compare it with that of a European. What might be different?

Surely, you can see some differences that distinguish a Japanese person from a person from the western hemisphere. Instead of falling into bad habits, they use virtues to stay true to their lives. In this way, the Japanese can be conscientious about their work and always look ahead. With a great deal of discipline, the Japanese live a structured life. You, too, can learn these virtues and put them to good use!

At this point, pick up a pen and ask yourself:

1. Which vices do you wish to overcome?
2. Which **virtues** can you embrace?

You have no doubt acquired some vices or bad habits in the course of your life. These are holding you back from professional and personal success, and you wish you could finally look to the future again. Japanese tradition and its virtues teach us that this is possible! Let us now take a look at the most important virtues cultivated by the Japanese:

DISCIPLINE

The Japanese take disciplined behavior to heart. We see this not only when they stand in line for a train or wait patiently at the ATM. You can also recognize discipline in the punctuality of the Japanese.

How disciplined are you?
Do you live in internal and external chaos, and do you fall back into your vices? Where can you be more disciplined?

FRUGALITY

The Japanese live frugally. This is not only reflected in their purchasing behavior. The Japanese also use only a few words, thus saving themselves further discussion. Frugality runs through Japanese everyday life: from the frugal use of words to their eating habits, the Japanese show us how it's done.

How frugal are you?
Where can you save more? Do you spend too much, or do you spend too much money on unnecessary things? Take a step towards yourself and be honest with yourself!

KINDNESS

In the Japanese tradition, kindness is vital. Japanese people are often mild and reserved in their behavior. They devote themselves to their work without complaining or claiming success for themselves. Instead, they keep a low profile and accept success without saying a word. They do not hold the belief that they possess superiority over others. We can observe this in the Japanese greeting when they bow to others—even in karate or judo competitions.

How much goodness do you have in you?

Do you always reach for success and want to let those around you know about it? Do you push yourself to the fore and always want to be first? Take a step back and see what happens.

HONESTY

Honesty is particularly evident in everyday working life when the Japanese conclude business deals. They know that dishonesty will not get them far and that it will affect their lives.

How honest are you?

Do you live behind a facade and hide, or can you express yourself freely? Do you do what you love, or do you do what is required of you? Be honest with yourself, and use this moment to decide what can change your life.

GRATITUDE

The Japanese are humble and grateful. Let us remember the people of Okinawa, who devote themselves to life and their everyday tasks. The Japanese accept everything with gratitude and know that life's difficulties and problems are also part of it.

How grateful are you?

Do you constantly complain, or can you go through the world with an open heart? Cultivate gratitude in your life by writing down three things you are grateful for every day (e.g., for your children, your morning tea, or your job).

Part 7: Self-reflection. Do the self-check!

Take a notebook and write it down:

- What virtues are you practicing?
- What are the obstacles that are hindering your progress towards achieving your objective?
- Which virtue would you like to incorporate into your everyday life?

For the next 7 days, write in your notebook every day to what extent you are practicing your virtues. What can you improve, and where are you currently?

8. Properties to avoid

"Our appointment with life
takes place in the present moment.
And the meeting point is right there,
where we are right now."
(Buddha)

How often do you mourn something? Maybe it's something you missed out on or a relationship that has come to an end. There are many situations in life that prevent us from living out of our ikigai. At the same time, we feel blocked from living a fulfilled and happy life. Many people tend to believe in their negative qualities. These include, for example, envy, hatred, and greed, as well as pessimism, materialism, and consumerism.

So what would it be like to take these characteristics by the scruff of the neck and stop believing them? Imagine, for a moment, a life without worries. Perhaps you feel free, unbound, and happy. This is precisely what the Japanese show us with their traditional way of life. By cultivating the virtues, they are less inclined to fall into bad habits. In this way, they can cultivate what is vital to them.

I would like to illustrate this with an example: imagine a person who wants to please everyone. I'm sure you know someone like this in your environment.

As long as this person intends to please everyone, they can neither find inner balance nor their Ikigai. The person will always live in imbalance. It is therefore important to shed light on the negative characteristics and avoid them as much as possible. How do you do this? I'll show you in just a few steps!

STEP 1: FIND YOUR BAD HABITS

Do you know the traits that you have been unconsciously cultivating for many years? These traits may lie deep in your subconscious, so they are not immediately apparent. So take a moment to look deep inside yourself. These traits are often hidden within us:

1. Anger and rage
2. Jealousy and envy
3. Hatred and greed
4. Grief after missed opportunities
5. Pessimism
6. Feeling that you have to please everyone.
7. Materialism

What can you find in yourself? By finding the trait, you can see how this trait is preventing you from being happy. All it takes is a moment of your time! Especially currently, we find more and more people controlled by envy and greed. Do something different and use the Japanese way of life.

STEP 2: DO SOMETHING DIFFERENT

Have you recognized the characteristics that prevent you from being happy? Then you can start with the next step. Starting today, do something that you don't normally do! Here are a few examples:

Be considerate. Keep the door open for the person behind you, even if you are hurrying.

Make time for the things you care about. Make time for a person who is indispensable to you, even if you have your work on your mind.

Stay calm. Talk to your boss about the problem that's bothering you instead of letting anger get the better of you.

Think of the people around you. Give the woman at the supermarket the last pack of cookies instead of buying two packs.

Find your inner balance. Only do what is in your hands, and don't overwork yourself. Learn to say no (e.g., at work).

STEP 3: THE 1-MINUTE RULE

Now it's time to put it into practice. We look at how you can manage the characteristics of your everyday life and be happier. To achieve this, we will use the 1-minute rule. This is based on the Japanese concept of Kaizen (see chapter 5). According to this concept, you only require one minute to adopt a new habit.

The advantage is obvious: you feel inspired to carry out the action because one minute is not long. This way, you can break old habits and do something you've always wanted to do instead (like learning a foreign language, doing sit-ups early in the morning, or doing a breathing exercise).

The short duration motivates you to take a new action and can thus awaken your inner impulse. By doing one minute of sit-ups or learning vocabulary every day, you will be inspired to do the same the next day. Over time, you will see that you invest more time in what you really want to do! In this way, you can trick your inner bastard, develop new habits, and give no space to negative traits.

Do something today that you've been wanting to do for a long time. (e.g., learn vocabulary, practice a yoga pose, or play an instrument) and make it a new habit!

Part 8: Self-reflection. Do the self-check!

Ask yourself the following questions and check which negative characteristics you have within you:

☐ When do you react out of frustration, anger, envy, or greed? Think back to a situation in which you reacted emotionally. How could you have reacted differently?

☐ When can you act differently than usual (e.g., by getting on a crowded train or doing your job)?

☐ What negative characteristic prevents you from being happy and satisfied (e.g., anger at your colleague or frustration about a missed deadline)?

9. Comfort Costs Progress

"If you're depressed, you're living in the past.
If you are anxious, you are living in the future.
When you are at peace,
you live in the present."
(Zen wisdom)

Living in your comfort zone means that you only ever do what you are used to. If you never go beyond the ordinary, growth is difficult.

We see this in many people who have successfully achieved their goals. This could be a marathon runner, a well-known artist, or a top chef in a gourmet restaurant.

They have left their comfort zone behind to achieve their goal.

Over the course of our lives, each of us acquires certain characteristics whose actions are transformed into habits. This can be excessive buying behavior or spending too much time with the wrong people, such as old childhood friends (see Chapter 12). Examples of bad habits that guarantee a comfort zone can be regular smoking or eating too much. But getting up late in the morning also ensures that we follow our old habits and the day follows a familiar pattern.

Habitual actions distract us from the opportunity to change something fundamental in our lives. If we look deeper, we can see that the actions are not the problem. Because it's the thoughts that make our comfort zone so cozy! There are certain thought processes and structures that we are used to. We can find this in the execution of our actions. I invite you to take a break from reading at this point and do some soul-searching.

1. Which thoughts are you listening to at this moment?
2. Which thoughts do you believe, and which do you not?
3. Which thoughts do you normally react to?

The reaction to a thought can be decisive in many moments of our lives. This is especially true when we want to escape our comfort zone. Here are a few examples:

Overweight: You know you are overweight and need to do something about your health. Instead, you continue to eat chocolate in the evening and eat too many large portions. By not believing the thoughts "Now a piece of chocolate" or "I need more," you can change the game in your favor. You will wake up fresher and more agile the next morning.

Dissatisfaction at work: You are dissatisfied with your work, and even talking to your boss doesn't bring about any change. However, instead of looking for a new job, you believe the thought, "I probably deserve it" or

"Maybe something will change at some point.". Again, disregard this thought and do something different. Take action and seek a new opportunity.

We see that habits start with a thought. Instead of reacting to this thought, say "no" from now on!

In every moment of your life, you have the opportunity to change your life and give it a new structure. I would like to illustrate this with a personal example:

When I was traveling, I had many opportunities. I could go anywhere, and yet at the beginning, I was influenced by my habits. I was used to staying in one place and living my life there—in my comfort zone. It was only after I met other travelers and saw that they were always visiting new places that I went beyond my comfort zone. I packed my backpack and, from then on, traveled to different places every week. I also left my permanent home behind, and this experience was also new to me. It changed my whole travel experience and thought structure!

Part 9: Self-reflection. Do the self-check.

Set yourself the following tasks for the next 7 days:

Take a bad habit and see what thought starts it.

☐ How strong are the thought and the stimulus to carry out this habit? Rank the habit on a scale of 1–10.

☐ Act differently: instead of reaching for a cigarette, pick up a book.

☐ By not following your usual routine, you can focus your awareness on the moment and feel it better. Ask yourself: What are my priorities at this moment?

☐ What change do you see when you don't believe your thoughts as usual?

10. Time Management

"Seek the silence and take the time and space to grow into your dreams and goals."
(Zen wisdom)

Our time on earth is limited. This makes it particularly precious. It not only includes a balanced lifestyle, such as getting enough sleep. Time is also an important factor that we humans should consider. For this reason, we should make the most of it and identify and eliminate all time wasters as far as possible.

It is not only critical to find the time wasters (such as spending too much time on social networks). You can also learn to prioritize your everyday tasks. This way, you will find more time for the things that are close to your heart! The more you do what you love, the happier you will be. At the same time, you will have more time for your family and friends and less time to spend on your work. The right prioritization will bring balance to everything in your life.

EISENHOWER MATRIX

The Eisenhower Matrix is a technique with which you can learn better time management. It is characterized by sorting your daily tasks into different categories. You can think of it like a drawer system. The main point is to transfer your tasks into a matrix and check their importance. In this way, various factors that limit your effectiveness (such as too many tasks or a lack of organization of your tasks) can be circumvented.

- In which categories can you categorize your tasks (e.g., household, office, family)?
- How important are your tasks in everyday life?
- How effective are you at completing your tasks?

POMODORO TECHNIQUE

With the Pomodoro technique, you divide your day into 25-minute intervals. There are five-minute breaks between each interval. This technique is designed to help you focus on the task in front of you. In this way, you avoid all distractions and can devote yourself to your tasks purposefully and effectively.

Ask yourself:

1. What distracts you?
2. What does your day look like in 25-minute intervals?

ROUTINES

Do you have routines in your everyday life, or do you let yourself flow with the daily routine? By giving your tasks a place in your day, you can dedicate yourself to them more productively. Clear space in your calendar and block out appointments for what is vital to you and what needs to be done (such as spending time with your family, going for a morning jog through the woods, completing your tax return, or filling out the paperwork for your self-employment). The more routine you have in your everyday life, the more successfully you can complete your tasks and successfully integrate new habits.

- How organized are you?
- Do you feel overwhelmed by life and by your tasks?
- What can you organize better, and where can you set a higher priority?

PARETO PRINCIPLE

The Pareto principle is based on the following fact:
20% of your effort is responsible for 80% of the result. Let's take a look at what this principle is based on:

- 20% of criminals are responsible for 80% of criminal offenses.
- 20% of drivers are responsible for 80% of car accidents.
- 20% of factories are responsible for 80% of pollution.
- 20% of a company's products account for 80% of sales.

It is clear that it is only 20% of your daily tasks that lead to true success. Find out what your key tasks are that contribute to your success. By avoiding the tasks that are less important, you can increase your success and gain more time for yourself!

- What are your key tasks?
- Which tasks can be identified as the most impactful (20%)
- What must happen that you take action and focus on these 20% key tasks?

SOCIAL MEDIA

Social networks are considered time-wasters. Even if you only want to reply briefly to a message, you spend more time than planned. Surely, you know this! Use social media only when necessary to save time. Set a daily limit for browsing social networks (e.g., 30 minutes) or only at a certain time (e.g., between 3 p.m. and 4 p.m.).

- How often do you look at your phone?
- How often do you actually need to look at your phone and use it?
- Which apps do you have that you spend too much time on?

Part 10: Self-reflection. Do the self-check.

Use the five methods for your success in life. Take the following questions to heart and use the five methods to find your true happiness in life:

☐ Which activities in your life are really necessary?

☐ Which activities are you successful with, and which activities are you less successful with?

☐ How much time do you spend on social networks every day?

☐ What routines would you like to incorporate into your life?

☐ How consciously do you live your everyday life?

11. Through Nostalgia into Happiness

A small light shines brightly,
gently warms your face.
Pain and sorrow fade away,
gloomy thoughts fade away.
The sweet scent of pine
in the air with you too.
Children's voices, bright and clear,
bells ring close by.
Dreams return
from a childhood full of happiness.
Christmas tales so close,
the way it used to be.

(Elke Bräunling)

Do you remember your childhood? Many people don't. We often repress the memories from our childhood and thus miss the opportunity to bring the child within us to life. But it is possible. The brain archives memories of experiences, allowing for future recall. This also applies to childhood memories. Even if you hardly remember your childhood, you can remember what you enjoyed at the time (e.g., riding a bike or climbing trees).

These may be stored in your brain, such as your first day at school, a fall on your bike, or your first visit to the zoo. You may also still be able to recall a trip on your summer vacation and feel emotionally connected to the place or the people. There are many such moments, and each person carries different experiences and memories.

Take your time to reflect:

- What do you remember from your childhood?
- What did you particularly enjoy in your childhood?
- When were you happy, and when were you unhappy?
- What did you not enjoy in your childhood?
- Which caregiver was particularly important to

you, and what role does this person play in your life today?

The deeper you look, the more nostalgic moments you can bring to light. Make a game of it and pick up poems like the one above to bring your childhood to life. It can also help to pause in your everyday life and let your childhood memories run free over a cup of tea.

The more you remember your childhood, the sharper your senses become. Smells, sounds, or a certain taste can bring back memories.

This can happen instantly when you are not expecting it. Relax, and embrace the moment.

Part 11: Self-reflection. Do a self-check!

Let the nostalgia and your memories have an effect on you over the coming days:

- ☐ Pay attention to your sensory organs and the stimuli from outside. What smell or taste awakens a memory in you?

- ☐ Is there something you are suppressing? Write down when you felt particularly good in your childhood and when you did not.

- ☐ How do you feel when nostalgic moments come to the surface? Do you try to distract yourself, or can you let your thoughts run free?

12. Personal Relationships

"If I let go of what is inside me, it will set me free;
If I hold on to what is inside me, it will destroy me."
(Zen wisdom)

Many people are held back from personal success by surrounding themselves with the wrong people. These can be friends, neighbors, or their family. Often, there is envy, jealousy, or simply a different perspective on life. It prevents these people from making the most of their lives. If you are surrounded by such people, you take on their characteristics. You start to accept what the people around you show you. There are numerous examples of what this can look like in everyday life:

- You live in a house with your parents. Your parents watch TV every evening and gripe about world events. It's no wonder that you are stuck in your life and look at everything negatively.
- You are in a relationship with a partner who constantly humiliates you. Instead of encouraging you, he only points out your weaknesses and downsides. This makes you feel small and discouraged.
- You regularly meet with friends who are getting nowhere in their lives. Your friends have become stagnant instead of seizing life's opportunities. Instead of pursuing their goals, nothing moves in their lives, and they remain empty words.

The more positive your social environment is, the more you can get out of your life. Remember how the inhabitants of the island state of Okinawa and the inhabitants of other Blue Zones live? Due to the harmonious way of life of all inhabitants, they always have people around them who encourage and support them. The more you adapt to your environment and orientate yourself towards people who speak clearly to you, the more you can find happiness in life.

Consider your social surroundings. You may have avoided this until now and believed that your friends would always support you. By taking a closer look at your social environment, you can find out which friendships are blocking you in your life and which friendships are helping you.

☐ Name five friends you admire for their qualities.
☐ What qualities do you respect or look up to in your parents or siblings?
☐ Is there someone in your family whom you look up to?
☐ Do you socialize with positive friends, or do they constantly complain?
☐ Name any friends who radiate negative energy.

As you delve deeper, you'll realize you're shaped by your social surroundings. Instead of continuing to cultivate old childhood friendships that hold you back from your goals, you should cultivate relationships with positive people. These can be friends who admire you for their way of life or strong qualities (e.g., the courage to do things differently from others or their creativity, spontaneity, and flexibility in life).

Friends who give you something in life are characterized in particular by the following qualities:

- ☐ They have a goal in mind and will do everything possible to achieve it.
- ☐ They don't let problems stop them, but they constantly seek an answer.
- ☐ They motivate you with your projects and plans.
- ☐ They support you morally and physically without trying to stop you.
- ☐ They are honest with you and point out both the positive and negative sides of a difficulty.
- ☐ They take time for you, and they know that your time is precious.
- ☐ They will not try to keep you from your goal or

project.

□ They are always available and will be by your side even in an emergency.

Do you know your true friends and the friendships you only have out of habit? The majority of people surround themselves with friends from their childhood, even if the friendships have long since fallen apart. Genuine friendships remain vibrant and forward-moving, rather than dwelling on the past. Therefore, let go of old vices and friends that you only meet out of habit.

Part 12: Self-reflection. Do a self-check.

Who are your true friends, and who is holding you back from success in your life? Use the following 3-day plan to help you analyze your environment:

Day 1: Who is your friend and who is not? Write down all the friends you can think of within 2 minutes. Then write down the positive characteristics next to each name. If you can't think of any positive qualities about the person, draw a line.

Day 2: A meeting between true friends: What do you do when a friend calls that you don't actually want to meet with? Do you have the courage to say "no," or do you meet with them out of politeness? Write down the names of the friends who steal your time.

Day 3: Who do you feel deeply connected to? Do you have friends with whom you live on the same wavelength? Maybe you know someone you admire but haven't been in touch with for a long time. Call this person and ask to meet.

13. Digital Detox

"If you're rushing, walk slowly."
(Asian proverb)

In today's era, we remain constantly accessible via our digital devices to connect with friends, family, colleagues, bosses, and customers. We hardly have a break for ourselves to devote ourselves to the true meaning of life. We drive along the highway at 112 miles per hour (ca. 180 km/h) with our headsets in our ears and feel stressed out by everyday life. This is what characterizes the modern life of an adult. How can we find our Ikigai like this?

Let's look back at the lives of the inhabitants of Okinawa. People spend most of their days working in nature. Fruit and fruit are harvested, vegetables and grains are grown, and leisure time is also spent among the rice fields. Smartphones and computer work do not play an important role there. On the contrary, the inhabitants smile at such a life dedicated to digital means.

Let's take another step back in time. Perhaps you grew up in a time when smartphones, laptops, and tablets didn't play a major role or didn't exist. We can hardly imagine such a time today. Many people's childhoods back then were characterized by children playing outside in nature a lot. They built massive sandcastles and explored the woods and gardens of their neighbors. It was a pure adventure!

Today, the adventure usually takes place on a digital screen. Perhaps you, too, feel drained by the constant accessibility and deadline pressure and are longing for a break. You can get this with a digital detox. Recently, the digital detox cure has become increasingly important, and the positive effects have become obvious: after just a few days, you feel more balanced and satisfied, and you have more time for the finer things in life.

An American study showed that 18% of US adults feel stressed by modern technology. Even teenagers admit that they are addicted to their mobile devices and check their messages every hour. Perhaps you feel similarly affected. Are you also unable to leave the house without your smartphone, constantly checking your emails, and never turning your phone off, even at night? Then it's time for a digital detox!

Take this test and see which statements you agree with:

- ☐ You feel anxious and stressed when you can't find your smartphone.
- ☐ You check your emails, apps, and messages every hour, or more often.
- ☐ You feel depressed, anxious, or stressed after surfing social networks for a long time.
- ☐ You pay a lot of attention to the likes, shares, and comments on your posts.
- ☐ You are afraid that you will miss something if you don't check your smartphone regularly.
- ☐ You spend late into the night playing on your smartphone and feel exhausted the next day.
- ☐ You can't concentrate on one thing and are distracted by looking at your smartphone.

How is your mental health, and to what extent are you affected by digital addiction? Be honest with yourself and observe your behavior. You can do a digital detox on your own. It will help you to reduce your everyday stress and get a healthier night's sleep.

Try detoxing today and make the following changes to your everyday life for the next 24 hours:

- ☐ Put your phone on airplane mode when you eat, walk, or sleep.
- ☐ Read a book instead of surfing on your phone or watching Netflix.
- ☐ Leave your phone turned off when you are doing a hobby or learning something new.

Once you have slowly become accustomed to the digital detox, you can also choose longer periods of time.

Perhaps there is a weekend when you want to switch off mentally, socially, and digitally. Then leave your smartphone switched off and feel the positive effects on Monday morning, such as a better night's sleep or a clear head. Here are some ideas on how you can prepare your digital detox cure:

- ☐ Tell your family and friends about your digital detox.
- ☐ Find a hobby to keep yourself busy during the detox period (e.g., painting, learning a language, or reading a book).
- ☐ Delete all social media apps on your smartphone to avoid temptation.
- ☐ Spend a lot of time outdoors in nature (e.g., jogging or walking).
- ☐ Meet with friends who are good for you and support you.
- ☐ Keep a diary in which you record your feelings and thoughts.

Part 13: Self-reflection. Do the self-check.

Are you ready to get started — without the temptation to look at your cell phone? Then use the digital break for yourself! If you're still not sure, you can ask yourself the following questions:

If you can answer the questions in the affirmative, it's time to take a break.

☐ Do you feel stressed all the time?

☐ Do you have trouble sleeping, or do you feel exhausted in the morning?

☐ Do you have a constant headache?

☐ Do you feel like you don't have time for the important things in life?

☐ Do you feel trapped in a hamster wheel?

14. Establishing Routines

„You are what you do every day."
(Aristotle)

Routines give us humans a certain sense of security in life. Routines are habits that we perform regularly and at a certain time. They can determine your eating habits, the way you dress, or your sports program. Whatever you plan to do in life, you can get a better grip on it with the help of a routine. Facebook founder Mark Zuckerberg, who wears the same T-shirt every day, knows this too. That way, he doesn't have to worry about what to wear in the morning.

Of course, this doesn't mean that you should only

wear one particular sweater. It's more about the idea behind the action. A routine is established to simplify your daily life. Routines also have another advantage: they help us to achieve our goals more easily and experience more happiness in life. For many people, bad habits have crept into their daily lives over many years (such as smoking or playing on their cell phones). But you can change these too and make positive habits part of your daily routine!

Identify routines that align with your life and desired goals. By defining your goal (e.g., losing weight), you can start your routine (e.g., running 5 times a week). You must proceed patiently and don't rush into anything. Take your time and make sure that you are still doing the new habit several weeks later. People often drop their new habits quickly and fall back into their old ones. By going slowly and being patient, you can successfully turn your new habit into a routine.

Answer the following questions and create your personal list of goals and routines on this basis.

1. What is my goal?
2. Is my goal realistic?
3. What routines can I establish to achieve my goal?
4. What motivates me to achieve my goal and maintain the routine?
5. Do I know someone who can support me?

I will give you a to-do list so that you are prepared for every situation. This will support you in your plan and on the way to your personal goal.

☐ Set a goal: Have one goal in mind instead of having multiple goals in mind.
☐ Choose a routine: Focus on routines that will help your reaching your outcomes.
☐ Avoid bad habits: Write down the things you would rather not do from now on.

□ Organize your calendar: Clear times in your calendar when you want to do your routine and focus on it completely.

□ Carry out an analysis: Make a daily note of your progress and keep a diary for the first three weeks.

□ Consider success: Once you have achieved your goal, move on and set yourself a new goal. Proceed in the same way again.

A daily morning routine can help you maintain your routines and make them easier to carry out. Get up early and do something you've always wanted to do. Whatever you do, focus only on that thing! To start the day fresh in the morning, you can plan your new routines the night before (e.g., a healthy breakfast or a cold shower in the morning). This will help to integrate your new habits.

Routines not only boost your creativity and productivity. You will also feel more energy, with which you can tackle any problem. Especially in stressful situations, you will be able to react more calmly and face the situation with more self-confidence. Do you have things that you enjoy doing? Then make a routine out of it, and you will see how this has a positive effect on your life!

Part 14: Self-reflection. Do a self-check!

Routines can only be integrated into everyday life if you approach them slowly and patiently. Once you have set your goal, the routine can be developed. The routine should be fun. Reflect on the subsequent questions to discover suitable daily routines:

What are you passionate about?
☐ Reading routine: 15 minutes of reading in the evening.
☐ Painting routine: 2 hours of painting on the weekend.
☐ Cycling routine: Cycling to work.

What do you miss in your everyday life?
☐ More peace and quiet routine: 5 minutes of meditation in the morning.
☐ Time with your family routine: Do something good for your family every day.
☐ Time for yourself routine: turn off your cell phone once a week and take a bath.

What stresses you out?
☐ Deadline pressure routine: take breaks between your appointments.
☐ The chaos in the office routine: organize your workspace once a week.

☐ Too many tasks routine: prioritize your tasks every morning.

What fills your heart with gratitude?

☐ For your family routine: Make regular contact with your family.

☐ For your life routine: Write down 3 things you are grateful for every day.

☐ The little things routine: Observe the little things (e.g., the butterfly in the garden) and say "thank you".

15. Less is More

"Not outside, only within yourself
one should seek peace.
He who has found inner stillness
reaches for nothing,
and he rejects nothing."
(Buddha)

You meet a friend who shows you his new smartphone. Shortly after the meeting, you also feel the urge to buy a new phone. Yet, your current smartphone is still functional and has no flaws. We can often observe similar behavior in other areas of life. We constantly compare ourselves with others and want to own what our colleague, friend, or neighbor has. This could be the neighbor's new car or the portion of spaghetti on the table next to you.

Such a desire can arise from one moment to the next. It is therefore important to observe it and not react to it immediately. Because what happens if you always react to the inner urge to buy something? Your four walls will be filled with things that you could have done without in the end, and you will regret your purchase. But a purchase has a much bigger impact. It's not just your head and wallet that are burdened. Every single purchase also affects the environment. The amount of plastic waste is immense, and nature suffers as a result.

By reducing your consumption, you can both better regulate your life and protect the environment. Instead of following a spontaneous buying thought, stop and ask yourself:

- Why do I need this?
- How often will I use it?
- How does my purchase impact the environment?

Instead of following your initial urge to buy, take your time. Let the thought fly through your head for a few days.

Remember the principle of Kaizen, in which patience is practiced? We use the Japanese principle here too: Wait five days instead of acting directly on your urge to buy. Has the urge to buy faded after five days, or has the thought taken root?

In modern times, we frequently miss the moment of true decision. We make snap decisions without much reflection when shopping. We regularly follow a single thought instead of taking the time to think about it. If we can consciously deal with the thought, we can see how true it really is. Let's take a closer look at this using a few examples:

- You walk past a bakery and smell the fresh bread rolls. Although you are not hungry, you buy several rolls and other baked goods.

- You see your colleague's new jacket in the office. As soon as you get home, you also want to buy a new jacket and look for a suitable jacket for yourself in an online store. Instead of just buying a jacket, you also order pants, sweaters, and other items.

- A friend tells you about the advantages of his new plasma TV over dinner. You feel motivated by the conversation with your friend to also buy such a TV. However, you do not normally attach great importance to a television. A few days later, however, you also have a large television with a Dolby surround system in your living room.

Take each of these situations and answer the questions above. You have a choice in every moment of your life. Do you make decisions on the spur of the moment that you later regret? A study in the UK in 2016 showed that 18% of food in British households ends up in the bin, and 30% of clothes bought go unused in the closet. The study also indicated that the majority of adults in the UK regret their purchases later (82%).

By limiting our consumption and living with less, we can also become more satisfied on the inside. We can follow the principle "As without, so within". The more things you own on the outside, the more thoughts you have in your head.

You can limit your consumption in all areas of life:

- Less water consumption (e.g., shorter showers).
- Less electricity consumption (e.g., turning off electronic devices when not in use).
- Less gas consumption (e.g., turning down the heating in winter when you leave the house).
- Less meat consumption (e.g., only eating meat one day a week).
- Less plastic consumption (e.g., fruit and vegetables without plastic packaging).
- less packaging (e.g., cook your food instead of having it delivered).
- less clothing (e.g., two pairs of shoes instead of ten pairs).
- Less CO_2 emissions (e.g., traveling by train instead of by car).

The more consciously you shop, the more you contribute to preserving the environment.

Part 15: Self-reflection. Do the self-check.

The less you own, the happier you can become. Try it out and change small things in your life.

- ☐ What can I consume less of (e.g., meat products)?
- ☐ What can I do every day to protect the environment (e.g., cloth bags instead of plastic bags)?
- ☐ What can I do without, and which things do I only buy out of habit (e.g., potato chips for TV evenings)?
- ☐ How environmentally friendly do I live?
- ☐ How consciously do I shop?
- ☐ When do I let my impulses guide me?

16. Focus

*"It's not relevant to be better than everyone else.
The important thing is to be better than you were
yesterday."*
(Japanese proverb)

It's easier to focus on the essentials in life. You will achieve more if you don't allow yourself to be distracted by small things. However, few people can focus on just one thing. There are daily distractions that make us forget our goal. You can also observe this in your everyday life:

You go to the kitchen to get a glass of water, and suddenly, your cell phone rings. Likewise, you answer the call and forget about the glass of water.

You have to finish a job but would rather spend the time watching a movie.

You want to rush to the supermarket to buy an ingredient for your lunch. Instead of just buying the missing ingredient, you come home with several shopping bags.

You will no doubt be familiar with these and similar examples from your everyday life. We humans have become used to doing numerous things at once.

This makes us forget what's happening right now. Early in the morning, we look at our cell phones over a cup of coffee and answer the first emails and phone calls. You could start the day in peace with your cup of coffee. Instead of enjoying it, we stress ourselves from one appointment to the next. Why is that?

We are dealing with a multitasking society today. We don't just do one thing; we do as many things as possible at the same time. If you observe your day, you too can see that you live in a multitasking culture. If we look at the people of Okinawa, we see the opposite. It is a life characterized by calmness and a focus on the essentials. How can you also perceive the essence of this moment? If you reduce your actions to the essentials, you too can find your way back to the moment. Start now and ask yourself: Are you reading these words carefully, or are your thoughts elsewhere?

113

Be honest with yourself and see where you can make a change. Here are a few examples:

- ☐ At breakfast, instead of playing on your phone and answering emails, savor every sip of your coffee and every bite of your cereal.
- ☐ At work, take one task to heart instead of doing several tasks at the same time.
- ☐ At a meeting, value your friends and give them your full attention instead of constantly glancing at your phone.
- ☐ On a walk, notice nature, listen to the birds chirping and watch the ducks in the lake.
- ☐ At dinner, savor every bite of your meal and taste the different flavors and spices.

The more you perceive the here and now, the more happiness you can experience. Because true happiness comes from within, not from doing many things at the same time. The more time you take to complete your tasks and give them your full attention, the more you can take a deep breath and be at peace with yourself. Multitasking has made us humans very jaded, especially recently. We have forgotten to appreciate the details in our work or the little things in life. Think back to Chapter 11 and how memories from your childhood can encourage you to simply be a child again!

Perhaps you enjoyed doing a jigsaw puzzle as a child, and you remember how you did nothing else for many days. Or did you enjoy drawing and didn't let anything or anyone get in the way? Then consciously seize this moment to do your work in this way or to achieve something that you have been meaning to do for a long time (e.g., painting the walls of your home).

Part 16: Self-reflection. Do a self-check.

What can you simplify in your everyday life, and where can you cut back? Take the following questions to heart and be aware of the present moment:

☐ Are you completing your tasks with full attention?
☐ Do you often have the feeling that you have to finish your tasks quickly?
☐ Is there anything that distracts you from your tasks (e.g., constantly looking at your cell phone)?

Take the Mindfulness Challenge for three days and get back into the moment:

Day 1: Raise more awareness

Get up consciously and focus your attention on your breath for the first few minutes of the day. Whenever you feel stressed that day, focus your attention on your inhalation and exhalation and make it a new habit.

Day 2: Focus on one activity

Turn it down a notch today and do everything more slowly than usual:

☐ Drink that cup of coffee after writing that email.

116

- ☐ Call your girlfriend after dinner.
- ☐ Finish reading the article before turning the page or jumping into another activity.

Day 3: Create breaks

Take conscious breaks in your everyday life. This can be a cup of tea in the office or a walk in the park. How about reading a book in the garden, or simply sitting and observing nature? Make the little things big and bring more contentment into your life!

What have you learned in these three days, and how do you feel? Write down what you want to take away from the last few days for the future, and what you intend to do without from now on. Make a conscious decision to adopt the new habits from now on and allow less stress.

17. Clarity

"Everything that we are
is created in our thoughts.
With our thoughts
we create the world."
(Buddha)

A clear head is often demonstrated by the fact that we also live in an orderly environment on the outside.

You can imagine this from a vivid example, such as Japanese culture.

The Japanese are characterized by their extreme cleanliness and tidiness. They leave no mess behind and always make sure that people feel comfortable in their surroundings.

The simplicity of things is given an important value.

You can see this in Japanese architecture, art, or technology. Through the orderly and clean execution of their work, the Japanese also find an inner order. Here again, you can remember the principle of "as without, so within". How can you sort out your life and make it simpler?

Perhaps you live in chaos, as I did a few years ago. Instead of listening to my Ikigai, I lived between a mess in my home and chaos in my office. I commuted like this for many years and wondered why I couldn't get a grip on my life. Follow your passions to create a more organized life. This was also the case for me, and I quickly realized after my life change that I felt more comfortable and could think more clearly in an orderly living and working environment.

How can you also sort out your areas of life and find more clarity? There are numerous routines and actions that you can use to start by sorting your external living environment. These include regularly tidying up, sorting papers on your desk, and dusting and cleaning surfaces in your living space. If your living spaces are clean, you will also feel cleansed inside.

Maintain cleanliness and tidiness at all times, and create a new habit. These tricks can help you:

- ☐ Spend 15 minutes every day tidying one part of your home (e.g., the drawers on your desk or a kitchen cupboard).
- ☐ Look at the rooms in your home and ask yourself, How comfortable do I feel here?
- ☐ Always tidy up after yourself when you leave a room (such as the office or bathroom).
- ☐ Focus on single-tasking to prevent chaos and clutter (e.g., do your work on the computer first and then take care of your tax return papers).

- ☐ Put everything back in its place after you have used it (e.g., put your shoes in the shoe cupboard, the book on the shelf, and the magazines on the waste paper).

☐ Sort your clothes, garbage, and all other household items by category (e.g., winter and summer clothes or waste paper, glass, and metal waste).

☐ Throw away items that you no longer need (e.g., clothes or jewelry that you no longer wear).

You will see that the more you tidy up the outer chaos, the more contentment you will find. The inner clutter is cleared, and you can feel freer.

In this new freedom, you are ready to make new plans, and you learn to focus on the essentials in your life (like becoming a self-employed web designer). You feel newly inspired and can find inspiration within yourself instead of looking for it in the outside world.

Part 17: Self-reflection. Do a self-check.

• Where can you tidy up your life? Start today! The following questions will help motivate and inspire you in your new living environment:

- What can you get done today instead of putting it off?

- Which area of your life is particularly unsorted? The outer areas of our lives are often symbolic of our inner thought structures.

- The basement represents the past and collects everything that is no longer needed.

- The attic represents the future and symbolizes the space we want to use in the future.

- The living areas represent the here and now. A life in chaos, order, and cleanliness.

- Minimize your household to the most necessary items.

Recycling:

— Put glass, paper, and old clothes in the appropriate containers.

— Classified ads: Place ads to sell old electronic devices, furniture, and clothing in good condition.

Practice „letting go". Say goodbye to the old and welcome more freedom and space in your life.

18. Have You found Your Ikigai?

"Blessed is the man who lives at peace with himself.
There is no greater happiness on earth."
(Buddha)

1= Abundant fulfillment without material wealth
2= Enthusiasm but uncertain
3= Okay, but a feeling of emptiness
4= Satisfied but feeling useless

Ikigai= Happiness. Intersection of all 4 circles.

Have you found your Ikigai or are you still searching? Finding your Ikigai is not about following a single concept. Rather, you learn to listen to your inner voice. Perhaps you have already been able to find more of yourself while reading this book, or you have decided that this will fundamentally change your life. Whatever it is — everyone has their path ahead of them. It is essential to find it and then follow it.

Use this chapter to answer the four fundamental questions of Ikigai for yourself:

1. *What do you enjoy doing?*

2. *What could the world need from you?*

3. *How could you earn money with it?*

4. *What are your strengths and talents?*

How have your answers changed from the beginning of this book to here? Compare what has changed and to what extent you have found your Ikigai. Those who know their strengths and weaknesses have an easier time in life and can achieve what they set out to do. With a sense of serenity, you can approach your tasks with humor and ease instead of stressing about them. With your Ikigai, you learn to earn money with an activity that you enjoy doing (e.g., working as a ski instructor in the Alps).

What was high up in the stars for you some time ago and seemed almost impossible to achieve, you can now realize. Instead of feeling small, you feel like you can embrace the whole world. Can you finally do what you were born to do? Then don't wait any longer and take each step with equanimity and ease. Always have an inner image of the Japanese in front of you, doing their work in silence and quietly celebrating their success. In this way, you too can soon celebrate your first success!

Part 18: Self-reflection. Do the self-check!

Ask yourself these questions and find out to what extent you have found your Ikigai: Are you doing what you are strong at?

☐ Are you doing what you are strong at?

☐ Are you self-assured in your abilities?

☐ Are you doing what you love?

☐ Do you feel fulfilled and happy?

☐ Are you doing something that benefits those around you and the world?

☐ Can you make a living doing what you love to do?

19. Exercises for more Mindfulness and Serenity

"Take care of every moment,
and you care for all time."
(Buddha)

We forget that there are many small things that carry great value.

Like the butterfly in the garden or a sunrise, we can pay more attention to the natural things in our lives again. This will help you rediscover the true wonders of life!

The following exercises will help you appreciate life's small moments. These mindful actions can bring a natural rhythm to your daily life.

Read through the exercises mindfully and start reading with more serenity. Let the words resonate with you and pick up an exercise every day that you can use to reshape your everyday life.

1. **Marvel at the small wonders.** Look around you and take the little things in life to heart (like a kind gesture from your colleague).

2. **Take a breathing break.** Take a break between the tasks in your everyday life and consciously focus on your breath for 2–3 minutes. Observe your breath, and then resume your work.

3. **Say "no if you don't have time or feel rushed**. In this way, you will find more time for what you enjoy doing.

4. **Ask yourself "why."** Take a moment that day and ask yourself:

    ☐ Why am I doing this thing?
    ☐ Why am I falling into this habitual trap?
    ☐ Why am I not happy?

5. **Spend time in nature:** A walk in the wood or a green park, will refresh your mind. Spent as much time in nature as possible.

    Eat slowly: Eat one meal a day and consciously take in every bite. What do you taste? Is the food bitter, salty, sweet, spicy, or hot?

    Say thank you: Say "thank you" regularly to yourself and to others. In this way, you can walk through the world more satisfied with every step you take. Take the gratitude diary with you and write down three things you are grateful for every day.

Do nothing: Drop everything and just do nothing for a minute. You will see that you may no longer be used to doing nothing.

Feel your senses.

- ☐ What do I hear?
- ☐ What do I see?
- ☐ What do I feel?
- ☐ What do I smell?
- ☐ What do I taste?

You can do this exercise when you are eating dinner in a restaurant, walking home through the streets, or doing your work at your desk.

Listen. Listen carefully to your friend or colleague instead of interrupting or nodding out of habit.

20. Further Japanese Self Improvement Concepts

USING SHIKITA GA NAI 仕方がない

TO SURMOUNT OBSTACLES

Unpredictability is a common feature of life. We frequently struggle with circumstances that are out of our control, which makes us feel frustrated and powerless.

This is where the idea of "shikita ga nai" in Japanese culture is helpful. This idea, which roughly translates as "it cannot be helped," encourages us to accept life as it is and use it as a strong tool to overcome obstacles and improve our wellbeing.

Acceptance

Shikita ga nai is anything but passive, despite the impression that it is a surrender to fate. Rather, it motivates us to accept the things we are powerless to alter while focusing our efforts on the things we can. This change in viewpoint has the power to transform.

Example: Let's say that you are stuck in traffic while traveling. Recognize that you have no control over the traffic, instead of allowing your frustration to mount as the minutes pass. Make use of this time to listen to a relaxing music. You'll use the time wisely and focus on developing serenity rather than tension.

Concentrating on Solutions

Accepting things as they are, allowing us to concentrate on taking constructive action. Being proactive gives us the ability to solve issues rather than focus on them.

Example: If you're overseeing a project at work and a critical team member abruptly departs, don't worry about the blow to your confidence; instead, rally the team that remains. Think of creative ways to divide up the work more efficiently, or even hire a temporary helper. By deciding to take on the task together, you'll promote cooperation and keep the project moving forward.

Developing Resilience

By serving as a constant reminder that obstacles are a part of life, Shikita ga nai promotes resilience. We learn to see setbacks as chances for progress, rather than letting them derail us.

Example: Let's take the case of an athlete who gets hurt right before a big competition. They can concentrate on their rehabilitation rather than regretting the missed chance. Establishing modest, doable objectives might assist them in regaining confidence and power. Every accomplishment serves as a springboard to return to its original form.

Reducing Stress

Attempting to manage the unpredictable causes stress for many of us. By teaching us to let go, Shikita ga nai helps us to reduce our worry.

Example: When you're getting ready for a big presentation and are concerned about any technical glitches, just focus on your preparation and delivery. Practice your main themes and make a backup plan for the arrangement of your presentation.

Developing Inner Calm

Shikita ga nai is about achieving inner calm amid chaos. We may cultivate a tranquil mindset by embracing the unpredictable nature of life.

Imagine: When adjusting to a new place or other personal change, concentrate on the opportunities rather than the risks. Investigate your new surroundings, make friends with the locals, and look for growth chances. Actively embracing the shift lessens your sense of uprootedness and aids in your adjustment to your new circumstances.

Conclusion

Using shikita ga nai gives us a strong strategy for overcoming obstacles in life with grace and resiliency. Accepting the things we cannot change and concentrating on our abilities gives us the strength to overcome challenges hastily. This kind of thinking encourages both personal development and a greater level of contentment in day-to-day living. Thus, keep in mind that there is nothing you can do to stop an unpredictable scenario from happening to you the next time. Instead, make the decision to actively and purposefully interact with life's obstacles.

OUBAITORI 桜梅桃李: BLOSSOM AT YOUR PACE

The Japanese idea of "oubaitori," which translates to "blossom at your pace," urges us to appreciate our unique growth paths in a world where success is frequently measured in terms of speed. It encourages us not to rush through experiences or compare ourselves to others, instead celebrating the idea that everyone has their timeline and rhythm in life. A life that is less stressful and more rewarding can result from comprehending and using this idea.

Oubaitori is derived from observing nature, particularly the cherry blossoms, or sakura, which bloom at specific times each year. This idea tells us that, just as flowers don't blossom all at once, we shouldn't feel under pressure to reach goals based on what other people think of us or how we compare to society. Real progress happens when our pathways, strengths, and circumstances match our own.

Benefits of Oubaitori

- **Less Stress and Anxiety:** We can become less stressed and anxious when we accept that it's acceptable to move at our pace rather than feeling pressured to keep up with others.
- **Enhanced Self-Awareness:** Oubaitori promotes reflection, which enables us to recognize our individual strengths and shortcomings and concentrate on sincere personal growth.
- **Sustainable Growth:** Rather than rushing to reach external standards, we nurture a more profound, lasting growth that is in line with our beliefs and objectives when we expand at our speed.

Oubaitori: Using It in Daily Life

Advancement in Career: Many people in work settings feel pressured to pursue awards or promotions quickly, gauging their success by the achievements of their colleagues. Rather, embrace the oubaitori mindset and concentrate on your personal development.

Example: If you want a promotion, but your

coworkers seem to be moving up the ladder more quickly, consider carefully improving your talents. Think about signing up for online classes or looking for a mentor. Cultivate mastery in your profession and develop personal goals that align with your values, rather than racing to cross off job titles.

Personal Development: We frequently base our personal objectives and New Year's resolutions on current events, which can demoralize us if we don't see results right away. Oubaitori shows us how to make goals for ourselves based on our readiness and desires.

Example: If you want to become in shape, set small, realistic goals that match your lifestyle first rather than forcing yourself to follow a rigorous exercise regimen right away. Maybe aim to walk for 15 minutes a day, and as your endurance increases, you could walk for longer. Appreciate every tiny accomplishment to keep yourself motivated and create a more profound bond with your fitness path.

Relationships: The social media landscape has given rise to countless comparisons between friendships, relationships, and lifestyles. Oubaitori exhorts us to value the distinct speed at which our interpersonal connections grow.

Example: If your friends' romantic relationships seem to be going faster than yours, concentrate on creating a strong foundation rather than feeling pushed to move things along too quickly. Spend some time connecting with people who share your interests and allowing the relationship to develop organically. This strategy may result in a more in-depth relationship.

Creative Activities: The pressure to create can inhibit creativity in any kind of self-expression, be it painting, writing, or any other creative endeavor. Oubaitori tells us that each person experiences inspiration and creativity uniquely.

Example: Allocate specific time to pursue your interest without expectations, rather than imposing strict deadlines on a creative undertaking. If you are writing a book, for example, instead of forcing yourself to write every day, make a goal to write a few hundred words whenever inspiration strikes. Your creativity can grow naturally with this fostering approach, producing more genuine work.

In summary

Oubaitori extends an invitation to all of us to accept our unique travels free from the burden of external expectations and comparisons. We may develop significant progress in many areas of our lives, lessen stress, and improve self-awareness by respecting our growth schedules. In the end, this idea is a subtle reminder that real blossoming occurs when we recognize the growth process, tune into our rhythms, and let each moment unfold wonderfully in its time.

HARAGEI 腹芸: JAPANESE SELF-IMPROVEMENT WISDOM

A lot can be lost in translation in our fast-paced, communication-driven world, both literally and figuratively. This is the Japanese idea of "haragei" at its best. Haragei, which means literally "belly technique," is a term that combines the depth of intuitive understanding, emotional intelligence, and the wisdom of nonverbal communication. It helps us develop empathy and reach a higher degree of awareness in our interactions, which might change the way we connect with ourselves and how we relate to other people.

Comprehending Haragei

Fundamentally, haragei highlights the importance of the hara, or lower belly, which is regarded in Japanese culture as a focus of vitality. People who establish a physical and emotional connection to this region can access their intuition and react to circumstances in a more genuine and grounded manner. In contrast to conventional communication methods that mainly focus on words, haragei promotes a more nuanced, intuitive style of speaking.

The Advantages of Haragei

Increased Awareness: Haragei increases awareness of your emotions as well as those of people around you. This comprehension can improve communication and strengthen bonds between people.

Enhanced Communication Skills: Our capacity to communicate grows more subtle and efficient as we develop our ability to interpret nonverbal clues and reply sincere.

Emotional Regulation: We may better control our stress and emotional responses if we embrace our intuitive impulses and establish ourselves in our bodies.

Stronger Bonds: By engaging in haragei, we strengthen our bonds with others by fostering empathy and trust, which fosters deeper cooperation.

Including Haragei in Daily Activities

Active Listening: Active listening, or paying attention to the sentiments that underlie words, is one of the core haragei techniques. Develop an openness that lets you feel their energy and emotions when they communicate to you.

Example: When conversing with a buddy, pay attention to their tone, expressions, and body language rather than formulating your answer as they speak. By listening more intently, you may reply more intelligently and establish mutual respect.

Body Awareness: Haragei invites us to establish a connection with our bodies, especially the hara. Our bodies provide us with a sense of grounding that allows us to access our instincts and intuition.

Example: Spend a few minutes every day focusing on your breathing. Put your hands on your stomach and take a comfortable seat. Take a deep breath and feel your belly grow. Breathe out slowly. This technique helps you focus yourself before making decisions or starting tough conversations, in addition to relieving mental tension.

Reading Non-Verbal indications: You can greatly improve your interactions with others by learning to read the subtle indications that people give out through their body language and facial expressions.

Example: Keep an eye out for other people's posture, eye contact, and gestures at meetings and social events. If a coworker appears uncomfortable or disengaged, think about changing your approach to be more understanding or inclusive to foster a more encouraging workplace.

Making Intuitive Decisions: By combining reasoning with intuition, you can significantly improve your decision-making process by utilizing the knowledge of haragei.

Example: Think things through before making a big decision, whether it's in your personal or professional life. Make a connection with your emotions on the given choice. Consider how each decision makes you feel physically. Are you tense, relaxed, excited, or afraid? Embrace these bodily experiences as insightful guidance during the decision-making process.

In summary

Haragei serves as a reminder that communication transcends language. We may increase our capacity for empathy and connection by learning to read between the lines of human contact and by becoming more conscious of our inner landscapes. By adopting this Japanese knowledge, we take a more profound path towards self-discovery as well as fostering our relationships with others. By integrating haragei into our daily lives, we can become more adept at navigating the intricacies of our emotions and relationships, which will ultimately result in a more contented and peaceful living.

Japanese Self Improvement Concepts in a Nutshell

Finally, I'd like to provide a concise overview of other Japanese philosophies.

1. Harmony (Wa, 和)

The concept of harmony permeates many facets of Japanese culture. It has to do with averting disputes and preserving harmony in interpersonal and communal ties.

2. Respect (Rei, 礼)

Respect is an essential value, especially for elders and other authority people. In everyday life, manners and politeness are reflections of this.

3. Mindfulness and Attention (Ichigo Ichie, 一期一会)

The phrase "unique encounter" highlights the singular nature of each moment. It inspires us to fully live in each moment and to cherish it.

4. Self-Reflection (Hansei, 反省)

Hansei, which translates to "self-reflection," is the act of considering one's past deeds to grow from mistakes and make constant progress.

5. Beauty in Imperfection (Wabi-Sabi, 侘寂)

The art of wabi-sabi is the ability to find beauty in impermanence and imperfection. It instills in us an appreciation for life's inherent simplicity and naturalness.

6. Mottainai (もったいない)

This idea encourages resource appreciation and respectful use while expressing regret over waste.

7. Gaman (我慢)

The term "gaman" refers to "perseverance" or "patience" and highlights the capacity to face hardship with composure and dignity.

8. Mono No Aware (物の哀れ)

This idea expresses a strong emotional response to the fleeting nature of things and their inherent beauty.

The Japanese way of thinking emphasizes **harmony, respect, and constant improvement** by fostering self-awareness, attentiveness, and acceptance of life's impermanence.

This is just a small excerpt from the Japanese way of thinking. If you would like to delve deeper, you will find further suggestions in the chapter **"Further Resources"** at the end of this book

Notes

In this area, you can give free rein to your thoughts. Use this space for yourself and the changes in your life. To give you a common thread, you will find six questions. You can use these to delve deeper into your Ikigai and live it in every moment. Take the chance and change your life — here and now!

The following 5-step plan will give you a common thread to help you let your thoughts flow. Let yourself be inspired by a Japanese saying:

"Even a journey of a thousand miles
begins with the first step."
-Lau Tzu-

1) What aspects of my life bother me the most?

_____

_____

_____

_____

_____

_____

_____

_____

2) What bad habits prevent me from finding my Ikigai?

3) What weaknesses would I like to eliminate (e.g., work on my figure, make more time for my partner, become more frugal, reduce media consumption, start a part-time job)?

_____

_____

_____

_____

_____

_____

_____

4) What do I enjoy doing the most? What are my strengths?

_____

_____

_____

_____

_____

_____

_____

_____

5) What specific actions can I define to stop points 1-3 and put point 4 into practice?

_____

_____

_____

_____

_____

_____

_____

_____

6) **Define a timetable: By when should the actions be implemented?**

_____

_____

_____

_____

_____

_____

_____

_____

Final Words

Life is like a journey. See every single day as an opportunity. In Buddhism, this is often symbolized by the lotus flower, which grows in murky waters and blooms with a hundred lotus petals. Your Ikigai will give you new energy and courage, allowing you to give your life meaning and shine from the inside out!

The Japanese philosophy of life, Ikigai, is like an inner motor that helps you balance your life and achieve your goals. Instead of continuing to follow old habits, you can change something in every moment of your life. It's like a fire that is lit from within and burns away all the things that are holding you back from your goals. Seize every moment and pause for several moments every day. What do you hear, see, and feel?

The more you use the Ikigai for yourself, the happier you will be. Even everyday actions such as drying the dishes or driving to the office will fulfill you. Use kaizen and improve your life to do what you love. Find a mentor who will constantly remind you from the outside what your goals are and how you can achieve them. It can be difficult to go it alone, especially at first. This makes the role of an idol or mentor even more important.

Once you have achieved the first goal, you will also successfully complete all other goals. Always stay harmonious with yourself and your values (such as patience, determination, and courage) and use small breaks in your daily routine to enjoy nature. Listen to birds singing or the sound of running water and take long walks. Consciously take time out to devote yourself to what you like to do (such as painting or playing the guitar).

Take your time and don't rush into anything. Take the Japanese inhabitants of the island state of Okinawa as your role model and live in serenity. Instead of letting your thoughts upset you, you can observe them and be more patient with yourself and other people. Live from the heart, and you will also influence those around you with your serene way of life.

We wish you a lot of serenity and patience with yourself and your fellow human beings on your journey through life. Pick up this book whenever you need it and consider it your silent companion on the path to your Ikigai.

"What lies behind us and what lies before us are tiny matters compared to what lies within us."
-Ralph Waldo Emerson-

Ikigai Certificate

Congratulations!

You have earned the Ikigai Expert certificate! This certificate certifies that you have understood the secret of Ikigai and can lead a fulfilling and satisfying life. You have learned how to harmonize your passions, talents, values, and needs to lead a meaningful life. We are proud to present you with this certificate and hope that it will motivate you to continue searching for your Ikigai and realizing your dreams.

About us

After several labor-intensive years as a permanent employee, Hiroto Niura found his Ikigai on a sabbatical. Exhausted by long working hours and excessive traveling, he longed for a break. He remembered his childhood and rediscovered his former passions. Today, he devotes himself exclusively to his passion, photography, and language teaching.

Patrick Hohensee is a publisher, author, and entrepreneur. He has traveled a remarkable journey from humble beginnings to a successful career. With a background in economics and extensive professional experience, including international corporations and start-up companies. He has a unique expertise in personal development, psychology, and resilience.

Inspired by his challenges (Job loss in February 2023 due to tech layoffs and 2 weeks later his father died), he aims to help his readers achieve their personal goals and stand their ground in difficult times. He found inner strength and peace in Buddhism and Stoic Philosophy.

Outside of writing, he is a passionate sportsman, nature lover and animal enthusiast.

Patrick's mission is to share inspiring, practical and encouraging content.

If you enjoyed this book, I would greatly appreciate it if you could take a moment to leave a **review on Amazon**. **Your honest feedback** not only helps others discover the benefits of this book but also supports my small business in a big way.

How you submit a review:
1. Visit the Amazon product page.
2. Scroll down to the 'Customer Reviews' section.
3. Click on 'Write a customer review.'
4. Rate the book and write your review.
5. Click 'Submit.'

Your contribution will make a world of difference, and I can't thank you enough for your support.

Thank you once again for being a part of this community of **growth and positivity**. Your words mean more to me than you know.

For any clarifications, comments, or ideas, please send an e-mail to: contact@patrick-hohensee.de

Explore my blog to learn more about personal development and asian philosophy:

https://www.patrick-hohensee.de/en/blog

Here you can delve deeper into further Japanese Concepts like **Kaizen, Wabi Sabi, Hansei and Shinrin Yoku**

Thank you for your trust and time!

Next Steps In Your Journey

The Uplifting Self Improvement Journal

Achieving Goals with Conscious Self Mastery.

Your Guide to Swift Personal Growth

Books that inspired us

1. The Cow who Cried: A Buddhist Tale of Compassion
2. The Tao of Warren Buffett: Warren Buffett's Words of Wisdom-Mary Buffett & David Clark
3. The Alchimist-Paulo Coelho
4. The Bhagavad Gita: A Walkthrough for Westerners-Jack Hawley
5. Marc Aurel-Meditations
6. Seneca-The Stoic Philosophy of Seneca: Essays and Letters

Further Resources

1. The Book of Five Rings by Miyamoto Musashi - A classic text on strategy, philosophy, and the way of the warrior, offering deep insights into Japanese thought.

2. Bushido: The Soul of Japan by Inazo Nitobe - An exploration of the samurai code and its influence on Japanese culture and philosophy.

3. The Art of War by Sun Tzu - While not exclusively Japanese, this ancient Chinese text has profoundly influenced Japanese strategic thinking and philosophy.

4. Zen and the Art of Motorcycle Maintenance" by Robert M. Pirsig - A philosophical exploration that, while not solely focused on Japanese philosophy, delves into the principles of Zen and mindfulness.

5. The Japanese Mind: Understanding Contemporary Japanese Culture" by Roger J. Davies and Osamu Ikeno - A comprehensive guide to various aspects of Japanese culture and philosophy, including Haragei.

More Resources on Wabi Sabi

1. Wabi Sabi: The Japanese Art of Impermanence" by Andrew Juniper
2. Wabi Sabi: Timeless Wisdom for a Stress-Free Life" by Agneta Nyholm Winqvist
3. The Wabi-Sabi House: The Japanese Art of Imperfect Beauty" by Robyn Griggs Lawrence

More Resources on Kaizen

1. Imai, M. (1986). Gemba Kaizen: A Commonsense Approach to a Continuous Improvement Strategy.
2. Maurer, R. (2004). One Small Step Can Change Your Life: The Kaizen Way.
3. Kato, I., & Smalley, A. (2010). Toyota Kaizen Methods: Six Steps to Improvement.
4. Imai, M. (1986). Kaizen: The Key to Japan's Competitive Success.
5. Narusawa, T., & Shook, J. (2009). Kaizen Express: Fundamentals for Your Lean Journey.

Ikigai Workbook

Welcome to Your 30-Day Ikigai Journey!

Congratulations on reaching this pivotal part of your Ikigai journey. This 30-day workbook is designed as a focused deep dive into **self-reflection and mindful discovery**—an invitation to actively engage with the principles and practices that help uncover your true purpose.

Throughout the book, you have already explored the concepts and practices of Ikigai. Now, it's time to turn inward with **renewed dedication and clarity**. Over the next 30 days, you'll embark on a journey guided by daily prompts crafted to help you reflect, recalibrate, and grow closer to your Ikigai. Each day offers you the chance to pause, reflect, and challenge yourself—whether through re-examining passions, aligning with your values, or exploring new perspectives.

Commit to this transformative process, be patient with yourself, and let each prompt reveal another layer of who you are and what you're meant to do. Remember, Ikigai is about embracing every part of your being—your passion, mission, vocation, and profession—in harmony.

Take a deep breath, open your mind, and begin this path of self-discovery with focus and an open heart. Your Ikigai awaits

Week 1: Self-Knowledge and Values

Day 1:

What makes you happy? Describe a moment when you felt particularly fulfilled.

_____

_____

_____

_____

_____

Day 2:

What values are most important to you in life? Why?

_____

_____

_____

_____

_____

_____

_____

_____

Day 3:

What skills or talents do you have that bring you energy and joy?

_____

_____

_____

_____

_____

_____

_____

Day 4:

Who are the people in your life who inspire you? Why?

_____

_____

_____

_____

_____

_____

_____

Day 5:

Which activities do you often put aside due to lack of time or fear, even though you enjoy them?

_____

_____

_____

_____

_____

_____

_____

Day 6:

Think of a time when you were proud of yourself. What did you do and what did you learn from it?

_____

_____

_____

_____

_____

_____

_____

Day 7:

Weekly reflection - What have you learned about yourself this week? What patterns do you recognize?

_____

_____

_____

_____

_____

_____

Week 2: Goals and Dreams

Day 8:

What are your biggest dreams and goals in life? Write down at least three.

_____

_____

_____

_____

_____

_____

Day 9:

What steps can you take today to get closer to your dreams?

_____

_____

_____

_____

_____

_____

_____

Day 10:

What obstacles stand between you and your goals? How can you overcome them?

_____

_____

_____

_____

_____

_____

_____

Day 11:

Who or what could support you on your journey? Make a note of possible resources and supporters.

_____

_____

_____

_____

_____

_____

_____

_____

Day 12:

What small successes have you already achieved? How can you build on them?

_____

_____

_____

_____

_____

_____

_____

Day 13:

Visualize your ideal day in five years. What are you doing? How do you feel?

_____

_____

_____

_____

_____

_____

_____

_____

Day 14:

Weekly reflection - How did your dreams and goals influence your week?

_____

_____

_____

_____

_____

_____

_____

Week 3: Profession and Vocation

Day 15:

What are your favorite tasks or activities in your current job?

_____

_____

_____

_____

_____

_____

Day 16:

What skills or knowledge do you have that make you stand out in your job?

_____

_____

_____

_____

_____

_____

_____

Day 17:

What are your professional goals for the next five years?

_____

_____

_____

_____

_____

_____

_____

Day 18:

In which moments do you feel particularly alive and engaged in your work?

_____

_____

_____

_____

_____

_____

_____

Day 19:

What aspects of your work bring you joy and fulfillment?

_____

_____

_____

_____

_____

_____

_____

Day 20:

Who or what inspires you in your professional environment? Why?

_____

_____

_____

_____

_____

_____

_____

Day 21:

Weekly reflection - What have you learned this week about your professional passions and goals?

_____

_____

_____

_____

_____

_____

_____

Week 4: Integration and implementation

(Mission and Vocation)

Day 22:

What positive impact do you want your work to have in the world?

_____

_____

_____

_____

_____

Day 23:

What problems or needs in the world are particularly close to your heart and how can you contribute to them through your work?

_____

_____

_____

_____

_____

_____

_____

Day 24:

What values do you want to embody in your professional and personal life?

_____

_____

_____

_____

_____

_____

_____

Day 25:

How can you use your personal strengths and talents to make a positive impact?

_____

_____

_____

_____

_____

_____

_____

Day 26:

What steps can you take to harmonize your professional and personal goals?

_____

_____

_____

_____

_____

_____

_____

Day 27:

What support or resources do you need to realize your mission and calling?

_____

_____

_____

_____

_____

_____

_____

_____

Day 28:

Weekly reflection - How have your insights this week changed your view of your professional and personal future?

_____

_____

_____

_____

_____

_____

_____

Day 29:

Review of the entire month - What did you learn about your Ikigai and your personal mission?

_____

_____

_____

_____

_____

_____

_____

Day 30:

Future steps - What concrete steps will you take now to live your ikigai and achieve your goals?

_____

_____

_____

_____

_____

Last Words from the Publisher

In our pursuit of Ikigai—the profound meaning and purpose of our lives—we can draw inspiration from the Bonsai tree. Like the Bonsai, discovering our Ikigai requires **patience, dedication, and continuous growth**. It is a process that unfolds over the seasons of our lives, teaching us to nurture ourselves with love and mindfulness.

The Bonsai symbolizes **harmony with nature**, and we too should strive to live in alignment with our values and passions. Ikigai is not merely about what we do, but how we do it—with **mindfulness, respect, and an open heart.**

Balance and equilibrium are at the heart of Bonsai artistry—and of life itself. Finding our Ikigai means achieving the **right balance** between vocation, passion, mission, and profession. It calls us to cultivate inner peace and grow with intention, seeking harmony within ourselves and with the world around us.

The care of a Bonsai embodies wisdom and profound spiritual meaning. Similarly, the journey to find our Ikigai invites us to pause, reflect, and focus on what truly matters. By approaching ourselves with care and awareness, we find the inner calm that allows us to live authentically.

The life cycle of a Bonsai reminds us to embrace **impermanence and cherish the beauty of each moment**. Our Ikigai is what makes us rise each morning with joy, what drives us to recognize the preciousness of every moment and live with dedication.

Ultimately, the Bonsai exemplifies the art of creating beauty and perfection on a small scale. Our Ikigai is the art of shaping our lives to reflect our unique talents and passions, seeing the beauty in simplicity.

The Bonsai stands for the endless process of self-improvement and the quest for our Ikigai. May you get inspired by the Bonsai, grow patiently—deeply rooted, harmoniously shaped, and full of wisdom.

With heartfelt wishes for your journey, may your path be filled with growth, balance, and profound purpose.

Warmly,

Patrick Hohensee

Further Notes

Made in the USA
Las Vegas, NV
27 December 2024

15392530R00125